The Adventures of Elli

ELLIE MEETS
THE NEW BABY

by Paula M. Karll

www.TrueVinePublishing.org

The Adventures of Ellie and Eve: Ellie Meets the New Baby
By: Paula M. Karll

Illustrations by: Shalini Saha

Published by True Vine Publishing Co.
P.O. Box 22448, Nashville, TN 37202
www.TrueVinePublishing.org

Copyright © 2021 by Paula M. Karll
ISBN 978-1-7357540-9-3

All rights reserved. No parts of this book may be reproduced, scanned, or distributed in any printed or electronic form without permission. Please do not participate in or encourage piracy of copyrighted materials in violation of the author's rights.

For more information about the author or to book for speaking engagements, visit author website: www.PaulaMKarll.com or contact Paula M. Karll at info@PaulaMKarll.com

Dedication

This book is dedicated to God, my daughters, Elise and Elaine, my dear husband, my parents, my parents-in-law, my siblings, nieces, nephews, and dear friends.

God, thank you for giving me the greatest gifts—my daughters—Elise and Elaine. They have inspired me and given me purpose to share our story. To my dear husband, who has been supportive of every aspect of me becoming an author and my journey. Thank you. To my parents, my parents-in-law, my siblings, nieces, nephews, and dear friends who have given me words of encouragement and inspiration during this process. Thank you. I will continue to cherish you all.

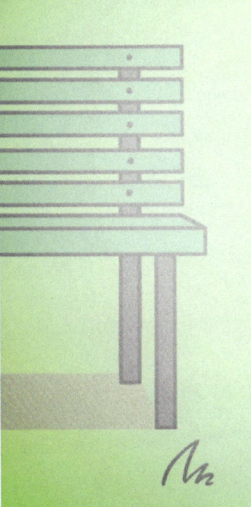

My name is Ellie Keen,
and I love to laugh and play.
I love to go to the park
and enjoy my dolls all day.

I also love to sing, dance,
and dress up in princess gowns.
I like to go outside and search
for creepy critters on the ground.

My mom will scream, "No Ellie!
You must put those critters down!
They are very gross and nasty!"
She would say with a frown.

Mom will have another baby soon.
She said it's going to be a girl.
I am so excited to meet her
when she comes into this world.

My beautiful sister, Eve, has arrived very early. She is so tiny and weak with lovely hair that is curly.

WAITING AREA

My mom cannot come home yet.
She must stay at the hospital, too.
This makes me so upset.
Now what am I supposed to do?

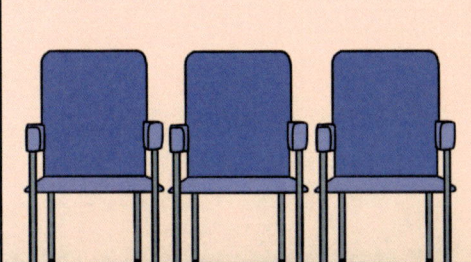

I say to her, "I love you.
Get well and come home soon."
But then Eve begins to cry.
It's such an annoying tune.

As Dad drives us home,
he notices my angry pout.
"What's wrong, Ellie?" he asks.
"I want my mommy!" I cry and shout.

"I have an idea," Dad says.
He knows how to stop my scream.
He turns the car around,
and says, "Let's go get ice cream!"

As I enjoy my strawberry swirl,
Dad says, "Ellie, you should be proud.
You are finally a big sister."
That makes me giggle and smile.

**Finally, Mom comes home.
I'm so excited she is here.
She picks me up and holds me tight
and says, "I've missed you so, my dear!"**

The next day, I ask Mom to play with me,
but Mom says, "Eve needs me now."
I guess we all live in Queen Eve's world,
for whom I have to bow.

I'd never felt so angry
before Eve came along.
Mom says, "Ellie, please stop complaining.
We must help Eve become big and strong."

Every time I look around,
there is something Eve needs.
Right now, it's her bottle,
which Mom gives her to feed.

When I want to snuggle with Mom,
she says, "Eve needs my arms to fall asleep."
This makes me so very sad.
I find a quiet place to weep.

"What's wrong, Ellie?" Dad asks.
"Mom has no time for me," I sigh.
"Eve this, and Eve that!
What about me?" I cry.

"That's not true, Ellie," Dad responds. "Eve is gentle and needs extra care." "But she gets all of Mommy's attention. I don't get any. It's not fair!"

Mommy hears Dad and me talking
and walks into where we are.
In her arms, she is holding Eve
who is sound asleep so far.

Mom puts Eve in her crib
and says, "Ellie, I love you so.
You should never doubt it.
This, I want you to know."

"You are a big sister,
and you are still my pride and joy.
But your baby sister needs us
to grow strong and have life to enjoy."

As I sit in bed, I think about
how I was once a baby, too.
I would cry, scream, and shout...
"I know what I will do!"

The next time Eve cries,
I will help Mom bathe her in the sink.
I will get Mommy a towel to dry
and make sure Eve doesn't stink.

When Eve needs her bottle,
I will get it for my baby sister.
She is becoming special to my heart.
When she is not around, I miss her.

Now, I enjoy my time with Eve
and will shower her with love.
I realize she is a blessing
from the heavens up above.

Name:_____

Reflections: Parents, take time to learn from your child's interpretation of the story. Ask your child each of the following questions.

1. What is the problem in this story?

2. What are some things Ellie likes to do?

3. What is Ellie so sad about?

4. How did Dad try to make her feel better?

5. What makes you feel better when you are sad?

6. What did Ellie realize that made her feel better about her sister?

7. How did Ellie show her love and understanding to her sister and Mom?

Name:_____

Draw a line through the maze to help Ellie reach Eve.

HELP ELLIE GET TO EVE

Name:_____

Describe Ellie's Faces: There are 5 faces of Ellie. Point to each one and ask your child to describe Ellie's facial expression.

Name:_____

Adventures of Ellie and Eve Crossword

DOWN:

1. Creepy things Ellie likes to search for

2. Eve needs extra what

7. What is the name of Ellie's baby sister?

Across:

3. Ellie is a big what?

4. What does Mom give Eve to feed?

5. What does Dad turn around to take Ellie to get?

6. Ellie believes Eve is a what?

Down: 1.) Critters 2.) Care 7.) Eve

Across: 3.) Sister 4.) Bottle 5.) Ice cream 6.) Blessing

The Adventures of Ellie and Eve

ELLIE MEETS
THE NEW BABY

For more helpful tips
visit our website:
www.PaulaMKarll.com